PAINTINGS
IN UNDER A
THOUSAND
WORDS

Nature Poems

SEAN M. TEAFORD

authorHOUSE®

AuthorHouse™
1663 Liberty Drive
Bloomington, IN 47403
www.authorhouse.com
Phone: 1 (800) 839-8640

Published by AuthorHouse   01/30/2016

ISBN: 978-1-5049-7638-1 (sc)
ISBN: 978-1-5049-7639-8 (e)

Library of Congress Control Number: 2016901682

Print information available on the last page.

This book is printed on acid-free paper.

Acknowledgements

The author would like to thank the following people: Dan Sklar, Harris Gardner, and Rhina Espaillat for their encouragement and support. My wife, Samantha, for never letting me forget about my writing. And, my son for providing me with the motivation to see this project to the end. These works would have never been possible without the help and support of these individuals.

Grateful acknowledgement is given to the editors of the following magazines in which these poems have appeared: *Mad Poets Review*: "How Long Does A Moment Last?" and *Endicott Review*: "Mobile Homes" and "Invisible Garden".

Other Works By Sean M. Teaford

Teaching a Stone to Talk: Nature Poems (Bending Tree Press, 2003)

Kaddish Diary (Pudding House Publications, 2005)

What Was Not Said: Echoes From The Holocaust (Author House, 2016)

Table of Contents

Preface

Many of the poems found in the following pages are all but memories of experiences that have colored my early life. Some see these moments as glimpses of a time past but I see them as paintings formed in slow deliberate strokes that highlight the details of life that instill the feeling of accomplishment when looking at your past. These images don't need the long drawn out descriptions laden with unnecessary letters, they are flashes quick to flood the mind and equally fast in fading back deep into the gray matter. This is why I see these poems, these memories of my encounters with nature, and paintings in under a thousand words.

Sand

From the depths of the ocean
small crustaceans gave up their lives
so we could burn our feet
on our way to the tide.

How Long Does a Moment Last?

The smell of the seaside stew-
a lingering sweet stench
of the sun baked crab
carcasses from yesterday.
The six-inch waves
crashed in muffled silence
like the folding of fringed,
ruffled bed linens.
The seagulls toed the rolls
like ballet dancers
as they glided
beyond the summits.
And as the bay water
faded on the beach,
it peeked around the rocks
like a little child-
wanting to go further,
needing to know more.

Companions

The high tide was gone
by the time we got to the beach
but, as a reminder,
it left its toupee on the sand.

The boaters didn't seem to care
as long as there wasn't a hole in the hull
and the buoys, unfazed,
floated on the Saran Wrap bay.

But the islands,
absent of Mermaids and Sirens,
bathed in the coastal air;
content on being exposed,
they continued their silent partnership
with cormorants.

Time and Tackle

With his brown Wolverine work boots
firmly supported on shells and moss,
he hovered above the rocks
and pools of sea foam mortar.

He cast over the green Atlantic blanket
and into the home of oil and fish.

There was not a single breath
to cradle the line from side to side
only the in and out sway of the waves.

When the stench of burnt sweat
began to flow through his nostrils
he knew it was time
to leave the tide to the seagulls.

Hot Chocolate and White Bread

Last night we stood on the beach,
stained by the oil brew bay tide,
like shards of splintered driftwood.
The moon's face was covered
by the cloud from the power plant stacks
like a marshmallow
disappearing in hot chocolate.

The cormorant witches swam
on the mirror-less water
forcing us to cast spell-laced bread
like yellow rescue rafts
in the hope that we could save ourselves.

Natural Diner

Speckled with the sun's
white rice gleams,
the waves rolled like sushi.
It was the freshest fish in town
but was still rejected
when the Salem power plant
was spotted across the bay.

The waiter was forced
to take the order back
hoping that the second plate
would be better.

Never satisfied, we were forced to wait;
the restaurant doesn't give refunds.

Mobile Homes

Shells, patterned like triangular springs,
laid half buried just beyond low tide-
the trailer park off the Bay Road
along the Atlantic Interstate.

Tornados never passed over the homes
of white trash hermit crabs
but the moon pulled the saline highway
several feet above their pointed roofs.

Rolling up, back and across the beach
they sank into their new neighborhoods
without their brother who was in pieces
just below the rocks- soon to be sand.

Without an anchor, without reaching higher ground,
before the sand dune mountains could be traversed
the waves will come and, inevitably,
the cinder blocks will only be out for a day.

An Atlantis Bride

The rose was tanned,
forgotten when it fell
from her charcoal hair.
Her pupils were heavy pebbles
in her green ocean eyes;
Her mind was lost,
uprooted from the sand.
Her voice gusts
slamming her body
against the rocks.
Her sensuous scent
evaporated
in the foaming mist.
Her memory lingered
as a rippling reflection.

Toiling Cormorants

There was a bay current caldron
above an island between four stones.

Cormorants chanted the day's spells below
the blue and white horizontal striped sky.

Stray waves destroyed the concoction,
just like every other brew,
making world domination impossible.

Bay Side View

The pitched lawn rolled harder
than the current drawn bay view.

The cliff beyond the stone fence
didn't leave much room for a beach chair.

But the cormorants didn't care
whether it was waves of water or grass.
They preferred to anchor the rocks
that hovered above high tide.

Old Rope

The coast was covered
with the workings of an hourglass.

Children, cradled
in their white walled innocence,
swung over their pool of
summer baptism.

Sheltered by a tee pee of leaves,
leaning against the vertical wood,
they waited for their turn-
getting a little bit older
with every pendulum motion.

Moths on the Summer Porch

The disappointment of moths
is that at first
they are thought
to be butterflies
in the shadows
of maroon light
but are inevitably shunned
when their dusty reality
is discovered.
And when wrapped
in the silk spider quilt
we realize that our pity
cannot save them.

Canopied Cathedral

He walked around the clearing
blessing every opened journal
with yellow ragweed flowers.

He stumbled on the neon moss
and slipped on the excrements
of the pine trees.

He took a sip of cold decaf coffee
and noticed laces running through
the tree's exposed feet-
providing home in earth and air.

Walking Back

Stained glass leaves,
above the dying branches,
softened the forest floor
with a green candlelight.

There was an aroma
of decomposing pine needles
thickening the air
where birdcalls traveled.

The fire pit had no ash,
only charred wood whose glow
had long since passed.

And I know that, just like
the fire and beer worshippers
who left their herbal butts
on the logs around the flaming cove,
I have to walk down
the same bouldered steps that we
both had to climb up to get here.

Heavy Morning Air

A thousand flies exhaled their final breath
in the late bitter minutes of fall,
causing the fog to slide deliberately
across the asphalt streams.

The vapor cotton clutched the nests,
laced like shoes between the railings above the water,
and dulled the needle headlights
of lazy cars bobbing over the speed bumps.

The cold sauna was welcomed,
massaging my lungs through a cigarette's glow.

As quickly as it came,
the ponds hazy thoughts were forgotten.

October Night

There was a noisy fog
during last nights fall full moon.
But the coastal horns
couldn't stop the rocks
from denting the sand.

The mile-long twine
of container cars
clacked on the tracks and
battered the determined weeds
pressing towards the opaque sky
from between the railroad ties.

My keys were ringing in my hand
just before I opened the whining door
to leave the echoing fog.

Late Fall Frost

The vaporous diamond dust
glowed on the grass-
each crystal a mirror
of blank white streetlamp light.

The onyx pond completed
the ying yang landscape.

But the echoing ripples
from the preflight geese
dissolved any possibility
of human balance.

The Pride of a Bird

The bird's sonic flight
led him to a window paned boom.
The recoil sent him back five feet
where two other birds dodged his thud.

I extinguished my Marlboro under my boot
and slid my hands under his wings.
They didn't flap.
I cradled him in my hand;
he was smaller than my palm.
I tried to comfort him
from this side of the linguistic barrier.
He seemed to calm down
over those fifteen minutes.
He needed to heal his concussed ego
so I placed him on a rectangle of hay
and walked inside for breakfast.

After a half an hour of eggs, pancakes and poetry
I went outside to smoke another cigarette.
I looked to see if the bird was still there.
He was in the same spot
where I slid him beyond my fingertips;
when he saw me
he flew away in acknowledgement.

Canadian Immigrants

The green leaves were knitted
within the Burdock towers.
The squirrel weaved in-between
the telephone pole plants
looking to collect enough nuts
for his winter starvation.

With a mouth full of luggage
he heads back to his skyscraper home-
just off the path surrounding the pond,
next to the brick scaled pump house.
While depositing his mundane sustenance,
he noticed the October invasion
of French-Canadian ducks.

But the squirrel had no time
to guard against the seasonal assault;
he had to search for more winter storage.

A Murder Surrounded By Strippers

The clouds were racing the birds today.
Without a place for the murder to land,
the fake grass determined the winner.

The Evergreens and rocks didn't care;
they were busy gawking
at their neighbor's nakedness.
But the fields surrounding
the plastic stadium carpet were blind,
hidden under the clothes of the strip tease trees.

Thoroughbred

Always hold a leaf
up side down
so the luck,
in the horseshoe like stem,
doesn't run out.

Tea and Leaves

When I lifted my window
the brick brown skeletal leaves
rolled down the blue carpet hallway.

My meticulously steeped Earl Gray,
already chilled by the fall wind
from my bedroom's eyes,
sat on top of my book of
Eighteenth Century American Poetry.

Before I could carry
my cup of English tradition
back to the kitchen for reheating
the tree deposited
one of its photosynthesis workers
into my cup of late afternoon ease.

Yard Work For Saturday

The trees seemed backwards
in the empty mirror night-
swaying up and down
rather than side to side.

The ocean gusts blew
into the west
from the Atlantic
side street bay.
But the wind stopped
when it reached
the sandy brick building
leaving piles of leaves
on its eastern wall
that will not be raked
until the weekend.

October Storm Night

Outside my wind propped front door,
the rain began to caress
the parked New England branded cars.

The moons razor like clarity
mocked the anti-Occam night.

And the fire tattooed Machiavellian leaves
obscured the simplicity of the asphalt
in their attempt to change the season.

Fall Wind

There is a psychedelic speed
to the clouds today
but the leaves,
entwined in the grass,
remained stagnant.

The trees neon fire glow
swayed in the Morse code gusts.

And the dirt,
fearful of fall's winter change,
regretted its despise
of once being summer dust.

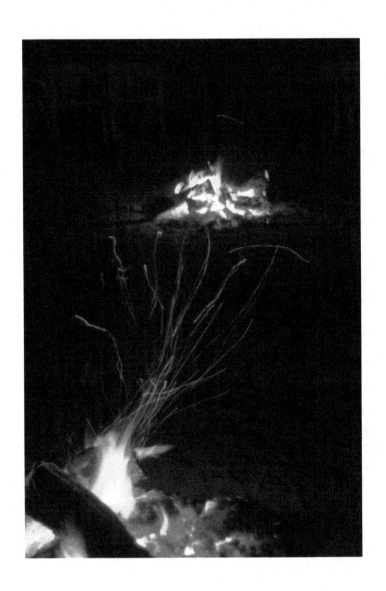

Drops and Grains

It was a damp day
on the brink of November.
It had rained that morning
but the wind had been
absent for about a week.

The last of the birds had left
during the previous low front.
The recent climb
into spring temperatures
reminded me of summer coulees
overgrown with weeds,
which had since withered away.

Leaves had reached
their seasonal plateau of change,
refusing in their ignorance
that winter was on its way.

The day light hourglass
continued to lose its grains
forcing us to wait longer
to turn it over for the next day.

Nature Music

The leaves hummed
in the inaudible breeze.

Needles dropped
from the trees
tapping the rocks
in a jazz drum beat.

The air got colder
without the sun.

It wouldn't be long
before winter came
and the snow
muffled the rhythm.

A Shrewish Season

The sun faded to amber
behind the ceiling's gray weave.

The clouds seemed sessile
during the past month
not allowing the quotidian zephyr
to shift the concrete shell.

Occasional rain
taunted me with its mirth,
confining me by creating a fall mire.

I tried to quash
the fall's obdurate hauteur,
but the pursuit was abandoned
when the first snow fell.

The Battle Between Seasons

The gale of missile rain glazed the grass
with its late fall fallout.

The disenfranchised trees dropped
their shelled humanitarian relief
and gliding kamikaze leaves.

But without the candle being lit,
the frozen water wax concealed
all efforts towards war and peace.

Cooking Weather

As the snow became rain
the air began to sizzle,
boiling the red-hot leaves
from their branches and
stewing the pock marked ground
into a vat of mud.

It cooked all morning
well below room temperature
until the carrot cut rays of the sun
faded beyond the horizon
and the freezer door was opened.

Falling Into Winter

The sapling rebels began their fall
anti-chameleon change;
the older, grander Poplars and Maples
stubbornly clutched what remained of spring,
what remained of their vitality.

The Evergreens didn't understand-
they only know of birth and death.
They welcome winter as a chance to shed
weak needles and brittle branches
while trying to bench press a blizzard.

But the grass remains absent
under the linoleum snow.

Rebellious Blizzard

The snow silently swayed
throughout the sky
bending between
the branches before
falling like a frozen felt
on the bitterly brittle
blades of grass.

The cars were caressed
with frozen flakes
while the sun
peeked through
the precipitation
offering a false
respite
from the impending deluge.

Bedroom Movie

The phone rang
at five thirty in the morning
startling his canine alarm clock.
When he picked up the phone,
Susan told him,
"classes are cancelled,
go back to sleep!"

He reached for his last cigarette
and slid the filter into his mouth.
He always smoked an unlit cigarette,
they were too expensive to light.

He rolled out of bed
like a wounded bird
and slowly made his way
to the brown folding chair
by the window.

The clouds had surpassed
the weatherman's predicted dusting-
the snow was falling thick and hard.

His window looked like
a screen in a movie theater
but with the speakers
and projector turned off.

Winter Night

Black snow silhouettes fell in front of
the apricot glow of the street lamps.

The trucks were coming around
on their first push of the night.
Each one had a yellow plow
checkered with missing flecks of paint
and exhaust burnt sleet.

Their shifted collection of cragged drifts
accumulated with every rapid succession
of scraping passes- depositing equal amounts
at the end of every driveway.

The sunrise never came that morning
but a steadily luminescent English overcast
wove the earth and sky into one
just like the ink black night before.

After The Snowfall

I had pushed the snow
into a plowed pile
but then I stopped
not wanting to lift my shovel.

My wool woven fingers
were cocooned with shattered ice.

I took a short cut
through the dormant garden
and when I got to the front door
I found that my hands
were cold and chapped
with brown burrs
hooked to my naked palm.

I had taken my gloves off too soon.

Second Snow

Bloated with their frozen overcoats,
the trees seemed to stop
in the regular flow of time.

Snow, falling straight down
in a mathematical efficiency,
transcended the moment
in their low-pressure drop.

My white on white polka dot
path from yesterday was now
only a collection of small valleys
between shaven winter hills.

In the Rockwellian fields
the only thing whiter
than the frozen fog
was my breath.

Late For Work

I dove into my pocket,
reaching for my car keys;
the bitter metal reflected winter.

The cold leather puckered my skin
as I turned the ignition.

Like a migrating bird,
the defrost gale
blew from north to south.

When the wallpaper fog faded
I pulled the shifter into drive
and slowly slid my foot
towards the floorboard.

But, without progress,
the tires began to screech and spin.

I was stuck again in the frozen mire.

Snow Traffic

The snow slowly rotated
as it fell to the crusted ground.

The lines painted on the road
had disappeared during the night
leaving a canvas in its place.

By late morning the asphalt roads
had become brown parallel paths.

And, between the rush hour winter ruts,
boot prints crisscrossed the invisible street
creating a collage of frozen leaves
not seen since fall.

Radio Cancellation

They sweat like freshly cut orange wedges;
ripe and sweet under their insulation from the snow.

No matter the bitter winter's overcast day
the adolescent surfs scaled the neighborhood mountain
dodging the screaming feudal overlords
as they bound down the hill in their Rubbermaid sleds.

Regardless of their sullen journeys down,
they flocked like migrating geese
when the time came for ascension.

They lived in the stain glass moment-
clear and colorful but they were oblivious to the day
waiting on the other side of the window pane.

With no snow in the nights forecast
the busses lay in wait perched on their chain laced feet.

Evolutionary Ditch

After the un-pigmented snow
faded into the clouds
the temporary mirror
reflected only black.

Seeping towards the bedrock,
the spring mud
teased disappointed mothers
with Lestoil dreams.

And in the midst of summer
the ditch cracked
like an ice cube in coffee.
That is the only time
when mothers and sons
welcome the rain.

Power Outage

There was a dark echoing glow
when Franklin's static child
was temporarily abandoned.

The candle bleached
the impurity of the sterile walls
with an orange hue.

As soon as the clouds
ceased their determined dripping
I obeyed nature's inaudible cry.
But the only one who could carry
this deliberate protest
was her felled fibrous son.

The Nature of Home

The blood letting of trees
has started prematurely
in between the lots
of baby boomer homes.

Leaves line the creek
after last night's rain
like the foam residue
left in a beer glass.

Deer tracks divide
the carpet of ambidextrous grass.

But the fox was absent,
resting in a spectrum-skinned gutter
beside Bryn Mawr Avenue.

The Trees Marked The Field

Back dropped with a porcelain blue drape,
canopies like rich royal green covered boulders
forming mountains in the sky.

Fur trees disguised with the color of money
in this white-collar neighborhood.

A leaning parceled fence like a highway divider-
one way on either side.

No feuds of territories
just lots of houses built only a score ago.

All sitting on what used to be rows of farmland
plowed by an old man on his big red tractor.

Discovered

Silence is the rustling of
Dogwood, Maple and Elm leaves,
the sound of clouds floating,
and the steady rhythm of rain
in the distance within me.

I pressed against my closed eyelids
and saw a shade of yellow
only found in the sun.

And when I covered my ears
I became enveloped in sheer darkness
and the distant falling waters
became rapids hovering below my feet.

Is this what Buddha felt
before enlightenment?

Smoke and Flowers

Blooming white orbs
on the outstretched
calloused and weathered
hands of Mother Earth-
They will be gone
within a week or two.

Tonight, I stared
at the dogwood tree
for the first time.

Even the purged
cigarette smoke
from my lungs
couldn't faze
my pupils.

But my mind drifted
as the moment fell
to my feet-

Zen passes in seconds.

Invisible Garden

Everyone forgets
a flower's shadow
and the grass
on which it projects.

Never casting
the same way twice
because
the only thing
more fleeting
than a flower
is its beauty
felled in a shadow.

Temporary Garden

The Tulip, curved
like the neck of a swan,
sat on the terrace table
as the third guest
between the conversations
of two empty chairs.

Independent of its roots,
the flower was forced
to rent the chipped
non-alcoholic carafe
until the last late office lunch
when the stale cologne and
six-dollar cigarette smoke
stripped it of its last piece
of wilted clothing.

Mars' Retreat

Above the opera crowd of
tobacco fiends and aristocrats,
like an orange and red
swirled marble suspended
from a seventh story clothes line,
Mars pierced through
the steam grate sky.

It didn't mean anything
hovering above Verdi's stage.

People didn't know what to think
as if they were reading
Roland Barthes' symbiotic theory
and contemplating the chair
on which the open book laid.

Why do you appreciate
the tie dyed planet
when it's so close
but never miss it
during its distance?

During the last probe
it was discovered
that huge lakes of ice exist
so, in preparation
of your two week stay
at the new Hilton Hotel
light years away,
remember to leave
your bathing suit at home
and stuff a pair of ice skates
in your duffle bag.

Tree

The sweat of Venus
pooled in her
hazel brown eyes
only to fall on
a yellow ribbon
being torn
from around
the waist of a
Pennsylvania Avenue
roadblock.

The Fate of an Environmental Flyer

A single leaf of paper
jaywalking across the street,
behind the fire engine,
and into the bloated
oil stained gutter
where passers by
glance down
and realize
there is nothing to read.

The Earth...

The earth does not need
independent funding;

The earth does not need
to sit through math class
to find the diameter of its equator;

The earth is happy with its body;

The earth does not need
to use an overhead projector;

The earth is not in the middle of the fights
between Mars and Venus;

The earth does not take drugs;

The earth makes drugs;

The earth doesn't groan
because of bad knees;

The earth is not a prostitute.

About the Author

Sean M. Teaford has honed a reputation for creating accessible and unforgettable images in his poetry. Over the past 15 years, Sean has published over 50 poems, articles, and photographs in numerous magazines throughout the United States and the United Kingdom including (but not limited to) The Endicott Review, The Mad Poets Review, Poetry Motel, Zillah, The Aurorean, Spare Change, Midstream Magazine, The Hypertexts, and others. His work was also included in the revised edition of Charles Fishman's anthology Blood to Remember: American Poets on the Holocaust and has been the subject of numerous reviews and profiles around the world.

Sean received a M.F.A. in Creative Writing from Rosemont College and a B.A. in English from Endicott College. He was Endicott College's nominee for the 2003, 2004, and 2005 Ruth Lilly Fellowships and won the 2004 Veterans for Peace Poetry Contest. In addition to serving as an editor for a variety of literary publications, including the Endicott Review and Mad Poets Review, he has coordinated numerous poetry readings across the Northeast and has been a featured reader in the Boston and Philadelphia areas.

In recent years, Sean has devoted his creative efforts to writing a daily blog, Time To Keep It Simple, which has served as his primary outlet for the observations, emotions, and reflections that can be found in the poetry that he still published on occasion. A public relations professional, avid genealogist, frequent traveler, and active mason, Sean lives in Morgantown, Pennsylvania with his wife and young son.

Printed in the United States
By Bookmasters